In the Woods

by Susan Green
Illustrated by Joanne Fitzgerald

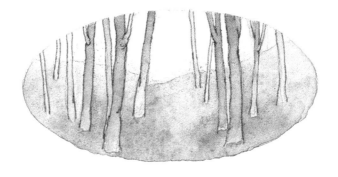

Dominie Press, Inc.

I went for a walk in the woods, the woods
I went for a walk in the woods.

Flowers fair were everywhere,
In the woods.

I went for a walk in the woods, the woods
I went for a walk in the woods.

A spider spun a web for me.

Flowers fair were everywhere,

In the woods.

I went for a walk in the woods, the woods
I went for a walk in the woods.

I saw three birds up in a tree.

A spider spun a web for me.

Flowers fair were everywhere,

In the woods.

I went for a walk in the woods, the woods
I went for a walk in the woods.

A busy bee went buzzing by.

I saw three birds up in a tree.

A spider spun a web for me.

Flowers fair were everywhere,

In the woods.

I went for a walk in the woods, the woods
I went for a walk in the woods.

I tried to catch a butterfly.

A busy bee went buzzing by.

I saw three birds up in a tree.

A spider spun a web for me.

Flowers fair were everywhere,

In the woods.

I went for a walk in the woods, the woods
I went for a walk in the woods.

Ants were marching to and fro.

I tried to catch a butterfly.

A busy bee went buzzing by.

I saw three birds up in a tree.

A spider spun a web for me.

Flowers fair were everywhere,

In the woods.

I went for a walk in the woods, the woods
I went for a walk in the woods.

I hear my father calling me...
It's hard to leave, it's hard to go.

When ants are marching to and fro.

I never like to say goodbye

To birds and bees and butterflies.

To spider webs and flowers fair.

All these things were living there,

In the woods.